ISBN 1-74022 425 6
Published by R&R Publications Marketing Pty. Ltd.
ABN 78 348 105 138

PO Box 254, Carlton North, Victoria 3054 Australia
Australia wide tollfree 1800 063 296
E-mail: info@randrpublications.com.au   Web: www.randrpublications.com.au

Publisher: Richard Carroll
Production Manager: Anthony Carroll
Cover Designer: Aisling Gallagher
Layout Designer: Elain Wei Voon Loh
Recipes: Concept New Zealand & R&R Kitchens
Photography: Concept New Zealand & R&R Kitchens
Proof reading: Chelsea Dunbar
Printed through Bookbuilders, Hong Kong

All rights reserved. No part of this publication may be reproduced or transmitted in any form or by any means, electronic or mechanical, including photocopying, recording, or any information storage and retrieval system, without permission in writing from the publisher.

Contents

Techniques	4
Savoury Muffins	6
Sweet Muffins	33
Cakes	49
Scones & Breads	90

Introduction

Nothing beats the taste of home-baked muffins, cakes and biscuits. Yet, today many people think of home-baked goodies as nothing more than a delightful memory. This need not be so. This book will show that not only is baking an easy and affordable way to fill lunch boxes and provide snacks for your family, but it is also fun. Here you will find a host of recipes that are easy to make and will bring those distant memories of mouthwatering freshly baked treats back to life. Baking has never been more fun than with this selection of quick and easy cakes and bakes. A bowl, a beater and a few minutes in the kitchen is all it takes to fill the house with the homely warmth and aroma that only a homemade muffin, cake or batch of biscuits can provide. So discover the pleasure of home baking and watch your friends and family return for more.

Techniques

When adding fresh fruit to batter it is best to follow the following advice: Whole berries and chopped fresh fruit are less likely to sink to the bottom of muffins and other quick breads during baking if you dredge them in flour first. Then shake off the excess flour in a colander before adding them to the batter. Besides helping to suspend the fruit evenly throughout the batter, the flour coating keeps moist pieces of fruit from clumping together.

The basic ingredients in muffins – flour, flavourings, perhaps some leavening, and liquid – are the same ones used in almost a dozen other varieties of quick breads. Creating such amazing diversity from a few common staples is largely a matter of adjusting the proportions of dry and liquid ingredients. Use two parts dry to one part liquid ingredients and you get a thicker batter for baking muffins or loaves. Thicker still, with a ratio of dry to liquid ingredients approaching three to one, are soft doughs for cut biscuits and scones.

Muffins and most quick breads are at their best when eaten soon after baking. Those that contain fruit, nuts, vegetables or moderately high amounts of fat stay moist longer than those that are low in fat. If muffins are left over it is best to place in the freezer in an airtight container, where they will keep for up to twelve months. To reheat, bake the frozen muffins, wrapped in foil, at 175°C for 15–20 minutes, or until heated through. You may also store quick breads and biscuits in the same manner.

Beer Muffins

3 cups flour
4 tsp baking powder
1 tsp baking soda
2 eggs
75g butter
355mL can beer

makes 12

1 Sift flour, baking powder and baking soda into a bowl. Make a well in the centre of the dry ingredients. Lightly beat eggs. Melt butter.

2 Pour eggs, butter and beer into dry ingredients and mix quickly to just combine.

3 Three-quarters fill greased muffin pans with mixture. Bake at 190°C for 15 minutes or until muffins spring back when lightly touched.

Carrot & Coriander Muffins

1 Mix flour, baking powder and salt together in a bowl. Rub cream cheese into dry ingredients. Lightly beat eggs. Make a well in the centre of the dry ingredients.

2 Mix carrot, coriander, eggs, milk and chilli together. Pour into dry ingredients and mix quickly to combine.

3 Three-quarters fill greased muffin pans with mixture. Bake at 200°C for 15–20 minutes or until muffins spring back when lightly touched.

1 cup wholemeal flour

1 cup flour

4 tsp baking powder

1 tsp salt

125g cream cheese

2 eggs

2 cups grated carrot

1/4 cup chopped fresh coriander

1 1/2 cups milk

2 tsp prepared minced chilli

makes 14

Cheese & Cornmeal Muffins

2 cups flour
4 tsp baking powder
1 tsp salt
1 cup fine cornmeal
2 cups grated tasty cheese
1 tsp dried basil
2 eggs
2 tsp prepared minced chilli
2 cups milk

makes 14

1 Sift flour, baking powder and salt into a bowl. Mix in cornmeal, cheese and basil. Make a well in the centre of the dry ingredients.

2 Lightly beat eggs, chilli and milk together. Pour into dry ingredients and mix quickly until just combined.

3 Three-quarters fill greased muffin pans with mixture. Bake at 190°C for 15–20 minutes or until muffins spring back when lightly touched. Serve warm.

Cheese Muffins

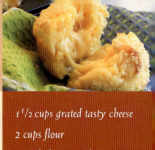

1½ cups grated tasty cheese
2 cups flour
4 tsp baking powder
¼ tsp salt
¼ tsp dry mustard
freshly ground black pepper
2 eggs
1¼ cups milk
¼ cup sesame seeds

makes 12

1 Place grated cheese in a large bowl. Sift in flour, baking powder, salt, mustard and freshly ground black pepper. Lightly beat eggs and milk together. Make a well in the centre of the dry ingredients.

2 Add egg mixture to dry ingredients. Mix until just combined. Three-quarters fill greased, deep muffin pans with mixture.

3 Sprinkle muffins with sesame seeds. Bake at 200°C for 12–15 minutes or until muffins spring back when lightly touched.

Walnut & Blue Cheese Muffins

100g wedge blue vein cheese

½ cup chopped walnuts

2 cups flour

4 tsp baking powder

1 tbsp sugar

2 eggs

1 cup milk

fresh pear slices

makes 30 mini muffins or about 12 regular muffins

1 Crumble blue vein cheese into a bowl large enough to mix muffins in. Add walnuts and mix. Sift flour and baking powder into the bowl. Stir in sugar.

2 Make a well in the centre of the dry ingredients. Beat eggs and milk together. Pour into dry ingredients. Mix until just combined.

3 Three-quarters fill greased, deep mini muffins pans or deep regular muffin pans. Bake at 190°C for 10–15 minutes for mini muffins, 20 minutes for regular muffins or until muffins spring back when lightly touched. Serve with sliced fresh pear.

John's Caper Muffins

2 cups four

4 tsp baking powder

½ tsp salt

50g butter

2 eggs

1 cup milk

100g jar capers

9 caperberries

makes 9

1 Sift flour, baking powder and salt into a bowl. Make a well in the centre of the dry ingredients.

2 Melt butter, lightly beat eggs and milk together. Pour butter and egg mixture into dry ingredients. Add undrained capers and mix quickly until just combined.

3 Three-quarters fill greased muffin pans with mixture. Place a caperberry into centre of mixture. Bake at 180°C for 20 minutes or until muffins spring back when lightly touched.

Low Fat Cottage Cheese Muffins

2 cups flour

4 tsp baking powder

1/2 tsp salt

1/2 tsp chilli powder

250g cottage cheese with chives

2 eggs

1 1/4 cups low-fat milk

makes 12

1 Sift flour, baking powder, salt and chilli into a bowl. Mix cottage cheese, eggs and milk together. Make a well in the centre of the dry ingredients. Pour in the cottage cheese mixture and mix quickly to just combine.

2 Three-quarters fill greased muffin pans with mixture. Bake at 210°C for 15–20 minutes or until muffins spring back when lightly touched.

Mexican Muffins

1. Sift flour, baking powder and salt into a bowl. Make a well in the centre of the dry ingredients.

2. Mix chilli into beans. Melt butter and mix in bean mixture. Lightly beat eggs and milk together. Mix in bean mixture. Pour milk and bean mixture into dry ingredients. Mix quickly until just combined.

3. Three-quarters fill greased muffin pans with mixture. Bake at 190°C for 15 minutes or until muffins spring back when lightly touched.

4. Serve warm with avocado slices, sour cream and tomato salsa.

2 cups flour

4 tsp baking powder

$1/2$ tsp salt

2 tsp prepared minced chilli

$1/2$ cup canned refried beans

50g butter

3 eggs

1 cup milk

To Serve
avocado slices, sour cream and tomato salsa

makes 11

Moroccan Couscous Muffins

½ cup couscous
½ cup boiling water
2 cups flour
3 tsp baking powder
½ tsp salt
1 tsp ground allspice
3 eggs
2 tsp grated orange rind
1¼ cups milk

makes 12

1 Soak couscous in boiling water for 5 minutes. Fluff up couscous with a fork. Sift flour, baking powder, salt and allspice into a bowl.

2 Make a well in the centre of the dry ingredients. Lightly beat eggs, orange rind and milk together. Pour into dry ingredients with couscous and mix quickly to just combine.

3 Three-quarters fill greased muffin pans with mixture. Bake at 190°C for 15 minutes or until muffins spring back when lightly touched.

Olive & Feta Muffins

2 cups flour

3 tsp baking powder

50g butter

1 egg

200g fetta cheese

1 1/4 cups milk

1 cup chopped, pitted black olives

1 tsp rosemary

makes 30 mini muffins, or about 12 regular muffins

1 Sift flour and baking powder into a bowl. Make a well in the centre of the dry ingredients. Melt butter. Beat in egg. Cut cheese into 1cm cubes.

2 Add butter mixture, milk, cheese, olives and rosemary to dry ingredients. Mix until just combined.

3 Three-quarters fill greased, deep mini muffin pans or deep regular muffin pans. Bake at 190°C for 10–15 minutes for mini muffins or 20–25 minutes for regular muffins, or until muffins spring back when lightly touched.

4 Serve warm, filled with cheese or pastrami.

Olive Tapenade & Anchovy Muffins

2 cups flour

4 tsp baking powder

50g butter

2 eggs

1/2 cup olive tapenade

1 cup milk

22 anchovy fillets

1/4 cup sliced black olives

makes 11

1 Sift flour and baking powder into a bowl. Make a well in the centre of the dry ingredients. Melt butter, Lightly beat eggs. Mix with tapenade and milk.

2 Pour butter and egg mixture into dry ingredients and mix quickly to just combine. Half fill greased muffin pans with mixture. Roll each anchovy fillet and place two fillets in centre of mixture. Top with muffin mixture to cover anchovies and three-quarters fill muffin pans.

3 Sprinkle with olive slices. Bake at 190°C for 15 minutes or until muffins spring back when lightly touched.

Pistachio Muffins

1 Sift flour, baking powder, cumin and salt into a bowl. Make a well in the centre of the dry ingredients. Melt butter. Melt butter. Lightly beat eggs and milk together. Pour egg mixture, butter and whole pistachio nuts into dry ingredients. Mix quickly until just combined.

2 Three-quarters fill greased muffin pans with mixture. Sprinkle with chopped nuts. Bake at 190°C for 15 minutes or until muffins spring back when lightly touched.

2 1/2 cups flour

5 tsp baking powder

2 tsp ground cumin

1/2 tsp salt

50g butter

2 eggs

1 1/4 cups milk

1 cup shelled pistachio nuts

1/4 cup chopped, shelled pistachio nuts

makes 12

Pizza Muffins

1 ham steak
3 cups flour
5 teapoons baking powder
1/2 tsp salt
1 tsp dried basil
1 tsp dried marjoram
2 tbsp tomato paste
1/2 cup olive oil
1 1/2 cups milk
1 cup grated mozzarella cheese

makes 12

1 Derind ham steak and cut flesh into small pieces. Sift flour, baking powder and salt into a bowl. Mix in basil and marjoram.

2 Bake a well in the centre of the dry ingredients. Mix tomato paste and oil together. Pour into dry ingredients with milk and ham. Mix quickly until just combined.

3 Three-quarters fill greased muffin pans with mixture. Sprinkle with grated cheese. Bake at 190°C for 15 minutes or until muffins spring back when lightly touched. Leave in pan for 5 minutes before removing.

Ploughman's Muffins

2 cups flour
4 tsp baking powder
50g butter
2 eggs
1 cup milk
1/2 cup Branston pickle
1/2 cup grated cheese

To Serve
ghekins
cheese slices

makes 12

1 Sift flour and baking powder into a bowl. Make a well in the centre of the dry ingredients.

2 Melt butter. Lightly beat eggs, milk and pickle together. Pour butter and egg mixture into dry ingredients and mix until just combined.

3 Three-quarters fill greased muffin pans with mixture. Sprinkle with grated cheese. Bake at 190°C for 20 minutes or until muffins spring back when lightly touched.

4 Serve with gherkins and sliced cheese.

Roasted Capsicum Muffins

2 red capsicums
2 cups flour
4 tsp baking powder
1 tsp salt
1 tbsp sugar
50g butter
2 eggs
1 cup milk

makes 12

1 Cut capsicums in half, deseed and place cut side down on an oven tray. Grill until skins are blistered and golden. Remove from oven, cool and remove skins.

2 Cut flesh into thin strips. Sift flour, baking powder and salt into a bowl. Stir in sugar. Make a well in the centre of the dry ingredients.

3 Melt butter. Lightly beat eggs and milk together. Mix butter, capsicum and egg mixture into dry ingredients until just combined.

4 Three-quarters fill greased muffin pans with mixture. Bake at 190°C for 15 minutes or until muffins spring back when lightly touched.

Satay Muffins

1 Sift flour and baking powder into a bowl. Make a well in the centre of the dry ingredients.

2 Melt butter. Lightly beat eggs and milk together. Mix in satay sauce. Pour butter and egg mixture into dry ingredients and mix quickly until just combined.

3 Three-quarters fill greased giant muffin pans with mixture. Sprinkle with chopped peanuts. Bake at 190°C for 15–20 minutes or until muffins spring back when lightly touched.

4 Serve warm filled with sliced lamb, salad greens and extra satay sauce.

3 cups flour

5 tsp baking powder

50g butter

2 eggs

1 cup milk

¾ cup satay sauce

¼ cup roughly chopped salted peanuts

To Serve
sliced cold lamb

salad greens

extra satay sauce

makes 12

Sesameal Muffins

2 cups flour
4 tsp baking powder
½ tsp salt
1 tsp ground cumin
2 tsp ground coriander
2 eggs
2 tsp grated lemon rind
1 ½ cups milk
½ cup tahini
2 tbsp toasted sesame seeds

makes 10

1 Sift flour, baking powder, salt, cumin and coriander into a bowl. Make a well in the centre of the dry ingredients. Lightly beat eggs, lemon rind, milk and tahini together.

2 Three-quarters fill greased muffin pans with mixture. Sprinkle with toasted sesame seeds. Bake at 190°C for 15 minutes or until muffins spring back when lightly touched.

Sundried Tomato & Basil Pesto Muffins

2 cups flour

3 tsp baking powder

2 eggs

1 cup milk

1/2 cup basil pesto

1/2 cup chopped sundried tomatoes

Parmesan cheese

makes 10

1 Sift flour and baking powder into a bowl. Make a well in the centre of the dry ingredients. Lightly beat eggs, milk and pesto together. Pour into dry ingredients with tomatoes. Mix quickly to just combine.

2 Three-quarters fill greased muffin pans with mixture. Bake at 190°C for 15 minutes or until muffins spring back when lightly touched. Serve slit with Parmesan cheese curls.

Swedish Potato Muffins

1 1/2 cups flour
3 tsp baking powder
1/2 tsp salt
50g butter
2 eggs
3/4 cup milk
2 cups grated potato
1/4 cup chopped fresh dill
1/4 cup chopped fresh chives
1/4 cup chopped parsley

makes 11

1 Sift flour, baking powder and salt into a bowl. Make a well in the centre of the dry ingredients. Melt butter. Lightly beat eggs. Mix with milk.

2 Pour milk and eggs, butter, potato and herbs into dry ingredients. Mix quickly to just combine.

3 Three-quarters fill greased, deep muffin pans with mixture. Bake at 200°C for 15–20 minutes or until muffins spring back when lightly touched.

4 Serve warm with sour cream instead of potatoes, rice, pasta or bread.

Tomato & Basil Muffins

2 cups flour

3 tsp baking powder

1/2 tsp salt

1 tsp sugar

3 tbsp oil from sundried tomatoes

2 eggs

1 cup milk

2 tbsp chopped fresh basil

1/4 cup drained sundried tomatoes in oil

makes 30 mini muffins or 12 regular muffins

1 Sift flour, baking powder and salt into a bowl. Stir in sugar. Make a well in the centre of the dry ingredients. Beat the oil, eggs and milk together until combined. Pour into dry ingredients. Add the basil and chopped sundried tomatoes. Mix until just combined.

2 Three-quarters fill greased, deep mini muffin pans or deep regular muffin pans. Bake at 190°C for 10–15 minutes for mini muffins, 20 minutes for regular muffins or until muffins spring back when lightly touched.

Mushroom Muffins

2 cups plain flour

1 tbsp baking powder

60g fresh mushrooms, chopped

$1/2$ cup cooked brown rice

$1/2$ cup shredded tasty (mature cheddar) cheese

1 tbsp parsley flakes

2 tsp chives, chopped

125g margarine, melted

1 cup/250mL milk

1 egg, beaten

Oven temperature 200°C

makes about 12

1 Sift flour and baking powder into a large bowl. Mix in mushrooms, rice, cheese and herbs.

2 Make a well in the centre of the dry ingredients. Add the remaining ingredients. Mix until just combined (see note).

3 Spoon mixture into greased muffin tins until three quarters full. Bake in the oven 200°C for 25 minutes. Remove from tin. Cool on a wire rack. Serve hot or cold.

Don't worry if not all the flour is incorporated as this gives muffins their characteristic texture. Sixteen strokes is usually enough when mixing.

Mini Sardine Muffins & Oat-bran Fruit Muffins

Mini Sardine Muffins

1 Combine flour, lemon thyme and paprika in a bowl. In a separate dish mix, together the egg, oil and milk. Quickly and lightly combine the dry and liquid ingredients. Fold in the sardines. Spoon mixture into lightly greased muffin pans or patty pans. Bake in an oven at 200°C for 12–14 minutes or until golden. Serve warm.

makes 24

1 1/2 cups self-raising flour

1 tbsp lemon thyme

pinch paprika

1 egg & 1/4 cup canola oil

3/4 cup milk

110g can sardines in tomato sauce, mashed

Oven temperature 200°C

Oat-bran Fruit Muffins

1 Combine flour, oat bran and brown sugar. Beat oil and eggs together and stir in the dry ingredients along with the fruit medley and buttermilk. Mix until just combined, do not over mix.

2 Spoon mixture into lightly greased muffin tins. Bake in an oven 190°C for 25–30 minutes.

makes 12

1 1/2 cups self-raising flour

1/2 cup oat bran

1/2 cup brown sugar

1/2 cup canola oil

2 eggs & 1/2 cup fruit medley

1 cup buttermilk

Oven temperature 190°C

Apple & Bran Muffins

1 1/2 cups wholemeal self-raising flour
1/2 tsp ground nutmeg
1/4 tsp baking powder
1/2 cup bran cereal, toasted
1/3 cup brown sugar
2 green apples, grated
2 eggs, lightly beaten
1/4 cup low-fat natural yoghurt
1 tbsp polyunsaturated vegetable oil

Oven temperature 180°C

makes 12

1 Sift together flour, nutmeg and baking powder into a bowl. Add bran cereal and sugar and mix to combine.

2 Make a well in centre of flour mixture. Add apples, eggs, yoghurt and oil and mix until just combined.

3 Spoon mixture into twelve greased 125mL muffin tins and bake for 15 minutes or until muffins are cooked when tested with a skewer.

The secret to making great muffins is in the mixing – they should be mixed as little as possible. It doesn't matter if the mixture is lumpy, while overmixing the mixture will result in tough muffins.

Apricot Oat-bran Muffins

1 Sift flour and baking powder together into a bowl. Add oat bran, apricots and sultanas, mix to combine and set aside.

2 Combine egg, milk, golden syrup and butter.

3 Add milk mixture to dry ingredients and mix until just combined. Spoon mixture into six greased 250mL capacity muffin tins and bake for 15–20 minutes or until muffins are cooked when tested with a skewer. Serve hot, warm or cold.

Serve this muffin for breakfast or brunch fresh and warm from the oven, split and buttered and perhaps with a drizzle of honey.

2 cups self-raising flour
1 tsp baking powder
1 cup oat bran
60g dried apricots, chopped
60g sultanas
1 egg, lightly beaten
1 1/2 cups buttermilk or milk
1/4 cup golden syrup
90g butter, melted

Oven temperature 180°C

makes 6

Cornbread Muffins

1 1/2 cups self-raising flour

1 cup cornmeal (polenta)

45g grated Parmesan cheese

1 tsp baking powder

1 tsp ground cumin

pinch chilli powder

2 cups buttermilk or low-fat milk

2 eggs, lightly beaten

1 tbsp polyunsaturated vegetable oil

Oven temperature 190°C

makes 12

1 Place flour, cornmeal (polenta), Parmesan cheese, baking powder, cumin and chilli powder in a bowl and mix to combine.

2 Make a well in centre of flour mixture, add milk, eggs and oil and mix until just combined.

3 Spoon mixture into twelve greased 90mL muffin tins and bake for 30 minutes or until muffins are cooked when tested with a skewer.

Cornmeal (polenta) is cooked yellow maize flour and is very popular in northern Italian and southern American cooking. It adds an interesting texture and flavour to baked products such as these muffins and is available from health-food stores and some supermarkets.

Potato Sour-cream Muffins

1 Place potato in a bowl. Add eggs, milk, sour cream and butter to the bowl and mix well to combine.

2 Combine flour and chives. Add to potato mixture and mix until just combined. Spoon mixture into six greased 250mL capacity muffin tins and bake for 25–30 minutes or until muffins are cooked when tested with a skewer. Serve warm or cold.

A properly cooked muffin should have risen well, be slightly domed in the middle (but not peaked!) and be evenly browned. It should also shrink slightly from the sides of the tin.

250g mashed potato

2 eggs, lightly beaten

1 cup milk

3/4 cup sour cream

60g butter, melted

2 1/2 cups self-raising flour, sifted

3 tbsp snipped fresh chives

Oven temperature 180°C

makes 6

Cheese & Bacon Muffins

4 rashers bacon, chopped

1 egg, lightly beaten

1 cup milk

¼ cup vegetable oil

2 tbsp chopped fresh parsley

2 cups self-raising flour, sifted

90g grated tasty (mature Cheddar) cheese

Oven temperature 180°C

makes 12

1 Place bacon in a frying pan and cook over a medium heat, stirring, until crisp. Remove bacon from pan and drain on absorbent kitchen paper.

2 Place egg, milk, oil and parsley in a bowl and mix to combine. Combine flour and cheese. Add flour mixture and bacon to egg mixture and mix until combined.

3 Spoon mixture into twelve greased 125mL capacity muffin tins and bake for 20–25 minutes or until muffins are cooked when tested with a skewer. Serve warm or cold.

An accurate oven is essential for successful baking. It should be well insulated and draught-proof, as a discrepancy of a few degrees can ruin baked goods. Regular checking with an oven thermometer helps avoid baking failures.

Blackberry & Apple Muffins

3 cups flour

5 tsp baking powder

3 eggs

1 1/2 cups apple juice concentrate

1 1/2 cups fresh or frozen blackberries

icing sugar

makes 12

1 Sift flour and baking powder into a bowl.

2 Make a well in the centre of the dry ingredients. Lightly beat eggs. Add to dry ingredients with apple juice concentrate and blackberries.

3 Mix quickly to just combine. Three-quarters fill greased muffin pans with mixture.

4 Bake at 190°C for 20 minutes or until muffins spring back when lightly touched. Serve dusted with icing sugar.

Banana & Mango Muffins

425g can mangoes in juice
2 over-ripr medium bananas
50g soft butter
2 eggs
¾ cup milk
¼ cup sugar
3 cups flour
2 tsp baking powder
1 tsp baking soda

makes 18

1 Drain mangoes, reserving juice. Chop mango flesh roughly. Pleace peeled bananas, butter, eggs, milk, reserved juice and sugar in a blender or food processor. Blend or process until fruit is pureed and mixture combined. Sift flour, baking powder and baking soda together.

2 Make a well in the centre of the dry ingredients. Add banana mixture and chopped mango and mix quickly until just combined.

3 Three-quarters fill greased muffin pans with mixture. Bake at 190°C for 20 minutes or until muffins spring back when lightly touched.

Blackberry Muffins with Yummy Blackberry Cream

1. Sift flour and baking powder into a bowl. Stir in sugar. Make a well in the centre of the dry ingredients. Melt butter and golden syrup.

2. Lightly beat eggs. Dissolve baking soda in the milk. Pour butter, egg and milk mixtures into dry ingredients. Add blackberries and mix quickly until just combined.

3. Three-quarters fill greased muffin pans with the mixture. Bake at 180°C for 20 minutes or untill muffins spring back when lightly touched. Serve warm, dusted with icing sugar and accompanied by blackberry cream.

Blackberry Cream

1. Mix blackberry juice, icing sugar and sour cream together.

Thaw frozen blackberries before using in this recipe. Chances are you will get some juice when the berries thaw. Use this for the cream or mash a few fresh blackberries to use for the cream.

2 1/2 cups flour

2 tsp baking powder

1/2 cup sugar

100g butter

1/4 cup golden syrup

2 eggs

2 tsp baking soda

1 cup low-fat milk

1 1/2 cups fresh or frozen blackberries

icing sugar

Blackberry Cream

2 tbsp blackberry juice or blackberry puree

1 tsp icing sugar

1/2 cup low-fat sour cream

makes 12

Honey & Fig Muffins

2 cups chopped dried figs
1/2 cup honey
100g butter
1 cup water
3 eggs
1 cup milk
3 cups flour
3 tsp baking powder
1 tsp baking soda

makes 17

1 Place figs, honey, butter and water in a saucepan. Bring to the boil and simmer for 5 minutes. Cool slightly.

2 Add eggs and milk and mix well to combine. Sift flour, baking powder and baking soda into a bowl. Make a well in the centre of the dry ingredients. Add fig mixture and mix quickly until just combined.

3 Three-quarters fill greased muffin pans with mixture. Bake at 200°C for 15 minutes or until muffins spring back when lightly touched.

Honey, Bran & Walnut Muffins

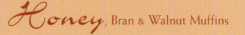

1 cup flour
1 tsp baking powder
$^1/_2$ tsp salt
$1^1/_2$ cups bran flakes
1 tsp baking soda
1 cup milk
1 egg
$^1/_4$ cup liquid honey
$^1/_2$ cup roughly chopped walnuts

makes 8

1 Sift flour, baking powder and salt into a bowl. Mix in bran flakes. Dissolve soda in milk. Lightly beat egg. Mix into milk with honey.

2 Make a well in the centre of the dry ingredients. Pour in liquid mixture and add walnuts. Mix quickly with a fork until just combined.

3 Three-quarters fill greased muffin pans with mixture. Bake at 200°C for 10–15 minutes or until muffins spring back when lightly touched.

Cappuccino Muffins

2 cups flour

3 tsp baking powder

½ cup soft brown sugar

¼ cup cream

1 egg

1 cup cold very strong black coffee

icing sugar

makes 24 mini muffins, or 10 regular muffins

1 Sift flour and baking powder into a bowl. Mix in brown sugar. Make a well in the centre of the dry ingredients.

2 Beat cream and egg together until combined. Pour into dry ingredients with coffee. Mix until just combined.

3 Three-quarters fill greased, deep mini muffin pans or regular greased muffin pans.

4 Bake at 190°C for 10 to 15 minutes for mini muffins or 15 to 20 minutes for regular muffins, or until muffins spring back when lightly touched. Dust with icing sugar to serve.

Use leftover coffee for this recipe. Mini muffins are an ideal size for a morning tea when other foods are being served.

Pineapple & Coconut Muffins

1 cup coconut

1/2 cup sweetened condensed milk

2 eggs

227g can crushed pineapple in fruit juice

2 cups flour

3 tsp baking powder

3/4 cup milk

makes 12

1 Mix coconut, condensed milk and eggs together until combined.

2 Mix in undrained pineapple.

3 Sift flour and baking powder into a bowl. Make a well in the centre of the dry ingredients.

4 Add pineapple mixture, egg mixture and milk. Mix quickly until just combined.

5 Three-quarters fill greased muffin pans with mixture. Bake at 190°C for 15 minutes or until muffins spring back when lightly touched.

Orange Sugar Cube Muffins

2 cups flour
4 tsp baking powder
1/4 cup sugar
100g butter
2 tsp grated orange rind
2 eggs
1 cup orange juice
12 sugar cubes

makes 12

1 Sift flour and baking powder into a bowl. Mix in sugar. Make a well in the centre of the dry ingredients. Melt the butter. Beat orange rind, eggs and orange juice together until combined.

2 Pour mixture into dry ingredients and mix until just combined.

3 Three-quarters fill greased muffin pans. Rub each sugar cube over the grated surface of the orange used for the orange rind.

4 Place a sugar cube in the centre of each muffin. Bake at 190°C for 15 to 20 minutes or until muffins spring back when lightly touched.

Choc-rough Muffins

1 Place butter and sugar in a bowl and beat until light and fluffy. Gradually beat in eggs.

2 Combine flour and cocoa powder. Add flour mixture, chocolate chips, coconut and milk to butter mixture and mix until just combined.

3 Spoon mixture into six greased 250mL capacity muffin tins and bake for 35 minutes or until muffins are cooked when tested with a skewer.

Muffin tins without a nonstick finish should be greased (and, if desired, also lined with paper baking cups) before use. Nonstick tins do not need lining but may need greasing; follow the manufacturer's instructions.

125g butter, softened
1/2 cup sugar
2 eggs, lightly beaten
2 cups self-raising flour, sifted
1/4 cup cocoa powder, sifted
155g chocolate chips
45g shredded coconut
3/4 cup buttermilk or milk

Oven temperature 180°C

makes 6

Sweet-Potato Muffins

375g sweet potato, peeled and chopped

½ cup wholemeal self-raising flour

1 cup self-raising flour

⅓ cup brown sugar

1 cup low-fat natural yoghurt

2 eggs, lightly beaten

1 tsp vanilla essence

3 tbsp currants

1 tsp ground cinnamon

Oven temperature 190°C

makes 12

1 Boil or microwave sweet potato until tender, drain well and mash. Set aside to cool.

2 Place wholemeal flour, self-raising flour and sugar in a bowl and mix to combine. Make a well in centre of flour mixture. Add yoghurt, eggs, vanilla essence, currants and cinnamon and mix until just combined. Fold sweet potato into flour mixture.

3 Spoon mixture into twelve greased 125mL capacity muffin tins and bake for 35 minutes or until muffins are cooked when tested with a skewer.

Make muffins when you have time and freeze them to have on hand for quick snacks. If you take your lunch to work, simply take a muffin out of the freezer in the morning — by mid-morning or lunch time it will be thawed.

Sticky Date Muffins

1 Sift flour, bicarbonate of soda and cinnamon together into a bowl. Set aside.

2 Place sugar, butter and dates in a saucepan and heat over a low heat, stirring constantly, until butter melts. Pour date mixture into dry ingredients, add egg and milk. Mix until just combined.

3 Spoon mixture into six greased 250mL capacity muffin tins and bake for 30 minutes or until muffins are cooked when tested with a skewer.

4 To make sauce, place butter, sugar, golden syrup and brandy in a saucepan and heat over a low heat, stirring constantly, until sugar dissolves. Bring to the boil, then reduce heat and simmer for 3 minutes or until sauce is thick and syrupy. Serve with warm muffins.

If 250 mL capacity muffin tins are unavailable, use the standard 125mL capacity tins and bake for approximately half the recommended time. The yield, of course, will be doubled. These muffins make a delicious dessert treat, but are just as good in lunch boxes and for snacks without the sauce.

2 cups self-raising flour

1 tsp bicarbonate of soda

1 tsp ground cinnamon

$1/3$ cup brown sugar

90g butter

125g chopped dates

1 egg, lightly beaten

1 cup buttermilk or milk

Brandy sauce

100g butter

$1/4$ cup brown sugar

1 tbsp golden syrup

1 tbsp brandy

Oven temperature 190°C

makes 6

Banana Choc-chip Muffins

1 large ripe banana
1 cup milk
1 egg
1/4 cup margarine, melted
1 1/2 cup self-raising flour
1/2 cup caster sugar
3/4 cup choc bits

Oven temperature 190°C

makes 12

1 In a mixing bowl, mash the banana, add the milk, egg and melted margarine. Mix well. Stir the flour, sugar and choc bits into the banana mixture, mix only until the ingredients are combined. Spoon mixture into well-greased muffin tins. Bake in an oven 190°C for 20 minutes. Serve warm or cold.

Classic Blueberry Muffins

1 Sift flour and baking powder together into a bowl, add sugar and mix to combine.

2 Combine eggs, milk and butter. Add egg mixture and blueberries to dry ingredients and mix until just combined.

3 Spoon mixture into six greased 250mL capacity muffin tins. Sprinkle with coffee sugar crystals and bake for 20–30 minutes or until muffins are cooked when tested with a skewer. Turn onto wire racks to cool.

Finely shredded orange peel can be added to this mixture to enhance the flavour of the blueberries. Coffee sugar crystals are coarse golden brown sugar grains. If unavailable, raw (muscovado) or demerara sugar can be used instead.

2 1/2 cups self-raising flour
1 tsp baking powder
1/3 cup sugar
2 eggs, lightly beaten
1 cup buttermilk or milk
60g butter, melted
125g blueberries
2 tbsp coffee sugar crystals

Oven temperature 200°C

makes 6

Blackberry Spice Muffins

½ cup self-raising wholemeal flour

½ cup self-raising flour

½ tsp ground allspice

¼ cup brown sugar

60g ground almonds

185g blackberries

1 banana, mashed

1 cup buttermilk

⅓ cup vegetable oil

1 egg, lightly beaten

Oven temperature 190°C

makes 12

1 Sift together wholemeal flour, flour and allspice into a bowl. Return husks to bowl. Add sugar, almonds, blackberries and banana and mix to combine.

2 Place buttermilk, oil and egg in a bowl and whisk to combine. Stir milk mixture into dry ingredients and mix until just combined.

3 Spoon mixture into twelve nonstick 125mL capacity muffin tins and bake for 15–20 minutes or until muffins are cooked when tested with a skewer. Turn onto a wire rack to cool.

If buttermilk is unavailable use equal parts of low-fat natural yoghurt and reduced-fat milk instead. These muffins are cooked in the large American-style muffin tins, however, if you prefer, regular-size muffin tins can be used. This recipe will then make 12–15 muffins and the cooking time will be 12–15 minutes. Alternatively ramekins or small pudding basins can be used to make large muffins.

Mango Bran Muffins

1 cup self-raising flour
2 tsp baking powder
1 tsp ground cardamom
1 cup oat bran
1/3 cup brown sugar
1 mango, chopped
2 egg whites
3/4 cup reduced-fat milk
1/4 cup vegetable oil

Oven temperature 190°C

makes 12

1 Sift together flour, baking powder and cardamom into a bowl. Add bran, sugar and mango and mix to combine.

2 Place egg whites, milk and oil in a bowl and whisk to combine. Stir milk mixture into flour mixture and mix well to combine.

3 Spoon mixture into twelve nonstick 90mL capacity muffin tins and bake for 15–20 minutes or until muffins are cooked when tested with a skewer. Turn onto a wire rack to cool.

When fresh mangoes are unavailable, drained, canned mangoes can be used instead.

Lemon-Poppy Seed Muffins

2 eggs, lightly beaten

1 cup sour cream

1/2 cup milk

1/4 cup oil

1/4 cup honey

3 tbsp poppy seeds

1 tbsp grated lemon rind

2 1/4 cups self-raising flour, sifted

Lemon cream-cheese icing

60g cream cheese, softened

1 tbsp lemon juice

3/4 cup icing sugar

Oven temperature 180°C

makes 6

1 Place eggs, sour cream, milk, oil, honey, poppy seeds and lemon rind in a bowl and mix well to combine.

2 Add flour to poppy seed mixture and mix until just combined.

3 Spoon mixture into six greased 250mL capacity muffin tins and bake for 25–30 minutes or until muffins are cooked when tested with a skewer. Turn onto wire racks to cool.

4 To make icing, place cream cheese, lemon juice and icing sugar in a food processor and process until smooth. Top cold muffins with icing.

A simple glacé icing is another suitable topping for muffins. To make, sift 155g icing sugar into a bowl, slowly stir in 3 teaspoons warm water and a few drops almond or vanilla essence to make a glaze of drizzling consistency. To vary the flavour, omit the essence and substitute the water with 3 teaspoons citrus juice or a favourite liqueur.

Apple Crumble Dessert Cake

1 Place butter and sugar in a saucepan large enough to mix all the ingredients. Hat, stirring, until butter melts. Beat eggs and milk together. Add egg mixture and sifted flour and baking powder to saucepan. Mix to combine.

2 Pour into a baking paper-lined 20cm cake tin. Arrange apple slices over cake, pressing the thin edge into cake. Sprinkle over topping.

3 Bake at 180°C for about 1 hour or until an inserted skewer comes out clean. Serve warm with softly whipped cream.

Topping
Peel apples. Cut into quartes, core then cut each quarter into 4 slices. Mix flour, sugar and baking powder together. Rub in butter until mixture resembles coarse crumbs.

125g butter
1 cup sugar
2 eggs
3/4 cup low fat milk
2 cups flour
4 tsp baking powder

Topping
2 granny smith apples
1/2 cup flour
2 tbsp brown sugar
1 tsp baking powder
50g butter

serves 6–8

Fruit Cake

2 cups dried mixed fruit
150g butter
1/2 cup brown sugar
1 tsp mixed spice
1 cup orange juice
2 eggs
1 3/4 cups flour
3 tsp baking powder

1 Place mixed fruit, butter, brown sugar, mixed spice and orange juice in a saucepan large enough to mix all the ingredients. Heat, stirring until boiling. Boil for 4 minutes. Leave to cool.

2 Using a wooden spoon, beat in eggs, flour and baking powder until combined. Spoon into a baking paper-lined 20cm round cake tin.

3 Bake at 150°C for 1–1 1/4 hours or until a skewer comes out clean. Leave in tin for 10 minutes before turning on to a cooling rack.

Never Fail *Sponge*

50g butter
3/4 cup sugar
1 cup flour
3 eggs
2 teaspoons baking powder
jam
whipped cream
icing sugar

1 Melt butter. Place in a mixer bowl with sugar, flour and eggs. Beat on low speed to combine then on high speed for 3 minutes. Stir in baking powder.

2 Pour mixture into 2 baking paper-lined 18 or 20cm sponge sandwich tins. Bake at 190°C for 15–20 minutes or until sponge springs back when lightly touched.

3 Leave in tins for 5 minutes before turning on to a cooling rack. When cold, spread one half with ham and whipped cream. Top with second half and dust with sifted icing sugar.

Rich Chocolate Cake

150g butter
1 cup hot water
1 tsp instant coffee
3/4 cup dark chocolate bits
1 1/4 cups sugar
3 eggs
2 tsp vanilla essence
2 cups flour
2 tsp baking powder
1 tsp baking soda
1/4 cup cocoa
icing sugar

1 Melt butter in a saucepan large enough to mix all the ingredients. Remove from heat and stir in hot water, instant sugar, stirring until dissolved.

2 Add eggs and vanilla essence and beat well with a wooden spoon until combined. Sift saucepan and mix to combine. The batter will be quite thin.

3 Pour mixture into a baking paper-lined 20cm square cake tin. Bake at 180°C for 50–55 minutes or until the cake springs back when lightly touched.

4 Leave in tin for 10 minutes before turning on to a cooling rack. When cold, dust with sifted icing sugar, or ice with chocolate icing.

Gingerbread

150g butter
1 cup low fat milk
1 cup golden syrup
½ cup brown sugar
2 tsp baking soda
2½ cups flour
2½ tsp ground ginger
2 tsp mixed spice

1 Place butter, milk, golden syrup and brown sugar in a saucepan large enough to mix all the ingredients. Heat until butter melts. Remove from heat and add baking soda.

2 When frothing stir in sifted flour, ginger and mixed spice. Mix until just smooth. Pour into a baking paper-lined 20cm square cake tin.

3 Bake at 180°C for 45–50 minutes or until the gingerbread springs back when lightly touched. Leave in the tin for 10 minutes before turning on to a cooling rack. Serve lightly buttered if desired.

Macaroon Cake

100g butter
½ cup sugar
3 egg yolks
1½ cups flour
2 tsp baking powder
½ cup milk
1 tsp vanilla essence
½ cup raspberry jam

Topping
3 eggs whites
¾ cup sugar
1½ cups coconut
1 tsp almond essence

1 Melt butter in a saucepan large enough to mix all the ingredients. Stir in sugar and egg yolks. Sift flour and baking powder into the saucepan. Add milk and vanilla essence and mix with a wooden spoon to combine. Spread springform pan or loose-bottom cake tin is best. Spread jam over batter. Spread over topping.

2 Bake at 180°C for 45–50 minutes or until an inserted skewer comes out clean. Cool in tin for 10 minutes before quickly inverting onto a clean teatowel-covered cooling rack, then turning onto another rack so topping does not get broken.

Topping
Beat egg whites until stiff. Gradually beat in sugar and continue beating until mixture is thick. Mix in coconut and almond essence.

Wholemeal Apple Cake

1 Place butter and sugar in a saucepan large enough to mix all the ingredients. Heat, stirring until butter melts. Remove from heat.

2 Beat in eggs and apple juice concentrate until combined. Mix in flours and baking powder using a wooden spoon, mixing until combined. Fold in canned apple.

3 Pour into a baking paper-lined 20cm cake tin. Bake at 180°C for 50–60 minutes or until cake springs back when lightly touched.

4 Leave in tin for 10 minutes before turning on to a cooling rack. Dust with icing sugar.

125g butter

½ cup brown sugar

2 eggs

¾ cup apple juice concentrate

1½ cups wholemeal flour

1 cup flour

4 tsp baking powder

410g can apple slices

icing sugar

Tosca Cake

125g butter

1 cup sugar

2 eggs

¾ cup milk

2 cups flour

4 tsp baking powder

Topping

50g butter

¼ cup sugar

70g packet sliced almonds

2 tbsp milk

1 Place butter and sugar in a saucepan large enough to mix all the ingredients and heat until butter melts. Remove from heat.

2 Beat eggs and milk together. Add to saucepan with sifted flour and baking powder. Mix with a wooden spoon until combined.

3 Pour mixture into a baking paper-lined 20cm round loose-bottom cake tin. Bake at 180°C for 45 minutes. Spread topping over and cook for a further 15–20 minutes or until the cake is cooked. Leave in the tin for 10 minutes before lifting out.

Topping
Place butter, sugar and almonds in a saucepan. Heat, stirring until the sugar melts. Add milk. Bring to the boil and boil for 5 minutes.

Cathedral Window Cakes

1kg mixed glace fruits such as pears, pineapple, cherries, apricots

350g blanched almonds

650g brazil nuts

9 eggs

1 1/2 cups caster sugar

3 tsp vanilla essence

1/2 cup brandy

2 1/4 cups flour

2 tsp baking powder

2 tsp mixed spice

makes 4 loaf-shapes cakes

1 Chop the glace fruits if large. Mix fruit, almonds and brazil nuts together. In a large bowl beat eggs, sugar, vanilla essence and brandy together. Fold sifted flour, baking powder and mixed spice into egg mixture. Mix fruit and nuts into egg mixture until combined.

2 Divide mixture evenly between four baking paper-lined 20 x 10cm loaf tins. Bake at 160°C for 1 1/4 hours or until an inserted skewer comes out clean. Cool in tins.

3 Remove lining paper and wrap in foil or seal in a plastic bag until ready to wrap for giving.

Raisin and Lemon Cake

1kg raisins
½ cup lemon juice
400g butter
4 eggs
2 cups sugar
2 tsp grated lemon rind
4½ cups flour
5 tsp baking powder
1 cup milk

1 Place raisins, lemon juice and butter in a saucepan large enough to mix all the ingredients.

2 Heat until butter melts. Cool slightly. Beat in eggs with a wooden spoon. Add sugar, lemon rind, sifted flour and baking powder and milk to saucepan. Mix until well combined.

3 Pour into a baking paper-lined 28 x 36cm roasting dish. Bake at 160°C for 1 hour or until cake springs back when lightly touched. Ice with lemon icing if wished. Cut into four cakes.

Linzer Cake

1 Place butter and sugar in a saucepan large enough to mix all the ingredients. Heat until butter melts. Cool slightly. Beat in eggs with a wooden spoon. Dissolve baking soda in milk. Sift flour, cinnamon, mixed spice and baking powder into saucepan. Add milk and mix with a wooden spoon until the batter is smooth.

2 Place half the mixture in a baking paper-lined 27 x 34cm roasting dish. Warm raspberry jam in the microwave or over hot water and spread over batter in tin. Sprinkle over walnuts. Top with remaining mixture.

3 Bake at 180°C for 1 hour or until cake springs back when lightly touched. Leave in tin for 10 minutes before turning onto a large cooling rack. When cold, dust with icing sugar and cut into four cakes or into squares.

250g butter

3 $1/2$ cups brown sugar

4 eggs

2 tsp baking soda

2 cups milk

4 $3/4$ cups flour

4 tsp cinnamon

2 tsp mixed spice

6 tsp baking powder

1 cup raspberry jam

1 cup finely chopped walnuts

icing sugar

Almond Cherry Cake

150g softened butter
¾ cup milk
3 eggs
¼ tsp almond essence
1 cup caster sugar
½ cup ground almonds
1½ cups flour
3 tsp baking powder
¾ cup chopped glace cherries
icing sugar

1 Place butter, milk, eggs, almond essence, caster sugar and almonds into the bowl of an electric mixer.

2 Sift flour and baking powder into the bowl. Beat on low speed for 1 minute. Scrape bowl down then increase speed to medium. Beat for a further 4 minutes. Fold in cherries. Pour mixture into a well-greased gugelhupf tin.

3 Bake at 160°C for 55–60 minutes or until cake springs back when lightly touched. Leave in tin for 10 minutes before turning on to a cooling rack. Serve dusted with sifted icing sugar.

Bowls Cake

1 Place butter, sugar, marmalade, raisins, vanilla essence and water in a saucepan large enough to mix all the ingredients.

2 Bring to the boil. Remove from heat and cool. Using a wooden spoon, beat in eggs, flours and baking powder.

3 Pour mixture into a baking paper-lined 22cm loaf tin. Bake at 180°C for 45–50 minutes or until an inserted skewer comes out clean. Leave in tin for 10 minutes before turning on to a cooling rack.

150g butter
1/2 cup brown sugar
2 tbsp marmalade
1 cup raisins
1 tsp vanilla essence
1 cup hot water
2 eggs
1 cup flour
1 cup wholemeal flour
4 tsp baking powder

Honey Cake

150g butter
½ cup brown sugar
½ cup honey
2 eggs
2 cups flour
3 tsp baking powder
1 tsp vanilla essence
icing sugar

1 Place the butter, sugar and honey in a saucepan large enough to mix all the ingredients.

2 Heat, stirring until butter melts. Remove from heat and cool slightly before beating in eggs, flour, baking powder and vanilla essence until mixture is combined.

3 Pour into a baking paper-lined 20cm round cake tin. Bake at 180°C for 45–50 minutes or until cake springs back when lightly touched.

4 Leave in tin for 10 minutes before turning out on to a cooling rack. Dust with icing sugar.

Banana Cake

150g butter
1 cup sugar
2 eggs
1 cup mashed banana
2 cups flour
1 tsp baking powder
1 tsp baking soda
2 tbsp milk
lemon icing

1 Melt butter in a mixer bowl in the microwave or over hot water. Add sugar, eggs and mashed banana. Mix on low speed to combine.

2 Sift in flour and baking powder. Dissolve baking soda in milk and add to the mixer bowl. Beat on low speed to combine. Increase the speed to medium and beat for 2 minutes.

3 Pour mixture into a baking paper-lined 20cm round cake tin. Bake at 180°C for 50–55 minutes or until cake springs back when lightly touched.

4 Leave in tin for 5 minutes before turning out on to a cooling rack. When cold, ice with lemon icing.

Lemon Sour Cream Cake

1¼ cups sugar
250g pot sour cream
3 eggs
2 tsp grated lemon rind
50g butter
1½ cups flour
1 tsp baking powder
1 tsp baking soda
icing sugar

1 Place sugar, sour cream, eggs and lemon rind in a mixer bowl. Melt butter and add to the bowl. Beat to combine. Sift flour, baking powder and baking soda into the boal. Beat on low speed until ingredients are combined. Increase speed to medium and beat for 3 minutes.

2 Pour mixture into a baking paper-lined 20cm round cake tin. Bake at 180°C for 35 to 45 minutes or until cake springs back when lightly touched.

3 Leave in tin for 5 minutes before turning on to a cooling rack. When cold, dust with sifted icing sugar.

Chocolate Apple Streudel Cake

1 Melt butter with sugar and cocoa in a saucepan large enough to mix all ingredients.

2 Remove from heat and beat in eggs and buttermilk. Sift in flour and baking powder and beat in with a wooden spoon until combined. Fold in canned apple.

3 Spread mixture in a 23cm square cake tin with a baking-paper-lined base. Sprinkle with topping and bake at 180°C for 1 hour or until an inserted skewer comes out clean.

Topping
Melt butter. Mix flour, brown sugar, baking powder, mixed spice and chocolate chips together. Mix butter through flour mixture until mixture is combined and crumbly.

125g butter
1 cup sugar
½ cup cocoa
2 eggs
¾ cup buttermilk
2 cups flour
4 tsp baking powder
410g can apple slices

Topping
50g butter
¼ cup flour
2 tbsp brown sugar
1 tsp baking powder
1 tsp mixed spice
½ cup chocolate chips

Chocolate Rum & Raisin Cake

¼ cup cocoa

¼ cup white or dark rum

150g butter

¼ cup sugar

3 eggs

1 ½ cups flour

2 tsp baking powder

1 cup raisins

1 Place cocoa, rum and butter in a saucepan large enough to mix all ingredients. Heat until butter has melted. Remove from heat then mix in sugar and eggs until combined.

2 Sift in flour and baking powder and mix until combined. Stir in raisins.

3 Pour mixture into a 20cm round cake tin with a baking-paper-lined base and bake at 180°C for 45–50 minutes or until cake springs back when lightly touched.

4 Cool in tin for 10 minutes before turning on to a cooling rack.

Chocolate Macaroon Cake

1 Melt butter in a saucepan large enough to mix all ingredients. Remove from heat and stir in sugar and egg yolks. Mix to combine. Sift flour, cocoa and baking powder into saucepan. Add vanilla and milk. Mix to combine.

2 Spread mixture into a 20cm ring tin. Spoon jam over cake batter and spread topping over. Bake at 180°C for 45–50 minutes or until an inserted skewer comes out clean.

3 Cool in tin before turning out onto a tea-towel-covered cooling rack. Turn back onto another rack so topping is on top.

Topping
Beat egg whites until stiff. Gradually beat in sugar and continue beating until mixture is thick and glossy. Fold in coconut, cocoa and almond essence.

100g butter

½ cup sugar

3 egg yolks

1¼ cups flour

¼ cup cocoa

2 tsp baking powder

2 tsp vanilla essence

½ cup milk

½ cup cherry jam

Topping

3 egg whites

¼ cup sugar

1½ cups coconut

2 tbsp cocoa

1 tsp almond essence

Café Cup Cakes

4 eggs
3/4 cup caster sugar
1 tsp vanilla essence
50g butter
1/2 cup flour
1 tsp baking powder
1/2 cup cocoa
2 tbsp instant coffee powder
6 x 4cm chocolate mint squares
icing sugar
finely grated chocolate

makes 12

1   Beat eggs, sugar and vanilla together until thick and creamy. The mixture will hold a 'figure-of-8' shape when it reaches this stage.

2   Melt butter. Sift flour, baking powder, cocoa and coffee into egg mixture and fold in with butter. Three-quarters fill greased muffin pans with mixture.

3   Bake at 190°C for 12–15 minutes or until cakes spring back when lightly touched. Cool in tins for 5 minutes before turning on to a cooling rack.

4   Cut a 1cm slit in the side of each cake. Cut chocolate mints in half diagonally and push cut side into cut in each cake. Dust cakes with icing sugar and decorate with grated chocolate as for a flat white coffee or a latte.

Chocolate Mousse Cake

1. Separate eggs. Beat yolks and sugar until pale, thick and creamy and the mixture holds its shape.

2. Beat egg whites until stiff. Melt chocolate and butter in a bowl over simmering water. Cool.

3. Beat into egg yolk mixture. Fold in the egg white. Line the bottom of a 20cm x 30cm sponge roll tin with baking paper and pour in one-third of the mixture.

4. Bake at 160°C for 35 minutes until set. Cool. Pour remaining mixture on top of the cake and freeze until firm. Garnish with chocolate curls and serve, if you wish, with whipped cream.

5 eggs
200mL brown sugar
100g dark chocolate
100g butter
chocolate curls

serves 6–8

Rock Cakes

2 cups self raising flour, sifted

1/4 cup caster sugar

90g butter

125g mixed dried fruit, chopped

1 tsp finely grated lemon rind

1 tsp finely grated orange rind

1 egg, lightly beaten

1/3 cup milk

1/2 tsp cinnamon mixed with

2 tbsp caster sugar

Oven temperature 180°C

makes 30

1 Place flour and sugar in a bowl. Rub in butter, using fingertips, until mixture resembles fine breadcrumbs. Stir in dried fruit, lemon rind and orange rind. Add egg and milk and mix to form a soft dough.

2 Place tablespoons of mixture on greased baking trays and spinkle lightly with cinnamon-sugar mixture. Bake for 12–15 minutes or until golden. Transfer to wire racks to cool.

Do not store different types of biscuits together as they will absorb flavours and moisture from each other.

Simple Chocolate Cake

1 Place the butter, sugar, and vanilla extract in a bowl and beat until light and fluffy. Gradually beat in the eggs.

2 Sift the flour, cocoa powder and baking powder together into a bowl. Fold the flour mixture and the milk, alternately into the egg mixture.

3 Pour the mixture into a greased and lined 18cm square cake pan and bake for 40 minutes or until the cake is cooked when tested with a skewer. Stand cake in the tin for 5 minutes before turning onto a wire rack to cool.

4 To make the icing, place the chocolate, butter and cream in a heatproof bowl set over a saucepan of simmering water. Heat, stirring constantly, until the mixture is smooth. Remove the bowl from the pan and set aside to cool slightly. Spread the top and sides of cake the with the icing and decorate with the dragees.

$1/4$ cup butter, softened
1 cup caster sugar
1 tsp vanilla extract
2 eggs, lightly beaten
1 cup all purpose flour
3 tbsp cocoa powder
$1 1/2$ tsp baking powder
1 cup milk
gold or silver dragees

Chocolate-Butter Icing
$1/2$ cup bittersweet chocolate
3 tbsp butter
$1/4$ cup double cream

Oven temperature 180°C

serves 8

Grandma's Chocolate Cake

½ cup butter, softened

2 cups caster sugar

2 eggs

2 tsp vanilla extract

1½ cups plain flour

1¾ tsp baking powder

5 tbsp cocoa powder

1 cup buttermilk

Chocolate Sour-cream Filling

1¼ cups bittersweet chocolate, broken into pieces

½ cup butter, chopped

3 cups icing sugar, sifted

½ cup sour cream

1 cup raspberry jam

Oven temperature 180°C

serves 10

1 Place the butter, caster sugar, eggs, and vanilla extract in a bowl and beat until light and fluffy. Sift together the flour, baking powder and cocoa powder.

2 Fold the flour mixture and the butter milk, alternately, into the butter mixture. Divide the mixture between 4 greased and lined 23cm round cake pans and bake for 25 minutes or until the cakes are cooked when tested with a skewer. Turn cakes onto wire racks to cool.

3 To make the filling, place the chocolate and butter in a heatproof bowl set over a saucepan of simmering water and heat, stirring, until the mixture is smooth. Remove the bowl from the pan. Add the icing sugar and sour cream and mix until smooth.

4 To assemble the cake, place 1 cake on a serving plate, spread with the jam and top with some filling. Top with a second cake, some more jam and some filling. Repeat the layers to use all the cakes and jam. Finish with a layer of cake and spread the remaining filling over the top and sides of the cake.

Chocolate Pound Cake

1 Place butter, sugar, and vanilla extract in a bowl and beat until light and fluffy. Gradually beat in the eggs.

2 Sift together the flour, baking powder and cocoa powder. Fold the flour mixture and the milk, alternately, into the butter mixture.

3 Pour the mixture into a greased and lined 10cm square cake tin and bake for 55 minutes or until the cake is cooked when tested with a skewer. Stand the cake in the tin for 10 minutes before turning onto a wire rack to cool.

This rich, buttery cake can be served plain, with a ready-made chocolate sauce or with cream. A simple glacé icing drizzled over the top makes another delicious alternative.

3/4 cup butter, softened
1 1/2 cups caster sugar
3 tsp vanilla extract
3 eggs, lightly beaten
1 1/2 cups plain flour
2 1/4 tsp baking powder
3 tbsp cocoa powder
1 1/4 cups milk

Oven temperature 190°C

serves 10

Chocolate-Hazelnut Torte

1 1/2 cups bittersweet chocolate, broken into pieces

6 eggs, separated

1 cup sugar

2 cups hazelnuts, toasted and roughly chopped

1 tbsp dark rum

caster sugar, sifted

Oven temperature 190°C,

serves 8

1 Place the chocolate in a heatproof bowl set over a saucepan of simmering water and heat, stirring, until the chocolate melts. Remove the bowl from the pan and let it cool slightly.

2 Place the egg yolks and sugar in a bowl and beat until thick and pale. Fold the chocolate, hazelnuts and rum into egg mixture.

3 Place the egg whites into a clean bowl and beat until stiff peaks form. Fold the egg whites into the chocolate mixture. Pour the mixture into a greased and lined 23cm springform tin and bake for 50 minutes or until the cake is cooked when tested with a skewer. Cool the cake in the tin and dust it with caster sugar just prior to serving.

Chocolate-Espresso Cheesecake

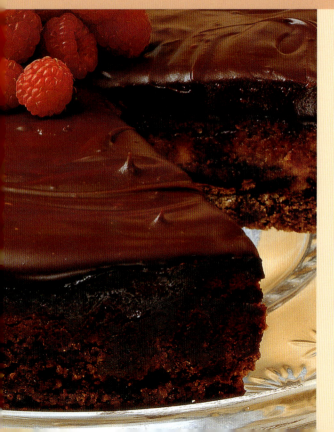

1 To make the base, place the biscuit crumbs and butter in a bowl and mix to combine. Press the mixture over the base of a lightly greased and lined 10cm springform tin. Refrigerate until firm.

2 To make the filling, place the coffee powder and water in a bowl and mix until the powder dissolves. Set aside to cool slightly.

3 Place the cream cheese, sour cream, eggs, sugar and coffee mixture in a bowl and beat until smooth. Pour 1/2 the filling over the prepared base. Drop 4 tablespoons of melted chocolate into the filling and swirl with a skewer. Repeat with the remaining filling and chocolate and bake for 40 minutes or until the cheesecake is firm. Cool in the tin.

4 To make the glaze, place the liqueur and rum into a saucepan and bring to simmering over a medium heat. Simmer, stirring occasionally, until the mixture reduces by 1/2. Add the chocolate, butter and cream and cook, stirring, until the mixture is smooth. Remove the pan from the heat and set aside until the mixture thickens slightly. Spread the glaze over the cheesecake and allow to set.

---

8 oz/255 g chocolate wafer biscuits, crushed

1/2 cup butter, melted

Chocolate-Espresso Filling

2 tbsp instant espresso coffee powder & 1 tbsp hot water

1 cup cream cheese, softened & 1 cup sour cream

3 eggs, lightly beaten & 1 cup caster sugar

1 cup bittersweet chocolate, melted

Coffee Liqueur Glaze

4 tbsp coffee-flavoured liqueur & 2 tbsp dark rum

1 1/2 cups bittersweet chocolate, broken into pieces

1/4 cup butter & 1/2 cup double cream

Oven temperature 200°C

serves 10

White Chocolate-Yoghurt Cake

1 cup white chocolate, broken into pieces

1 1/2 cups plain flour

1 cup caster sugar

2 eggs, lightly beaten

1 cup plain yoghurt

3 tbsp butter, melted

White Chocolate Icing

1/2 cup white chocolate

1 tbsp double cream

Oven temperature 180°C,

serves 6–8

1 Place the chocolate in a heatproof bowl set over a saucepan of simmering water and heat, stirring, until smooth. Remove the bowl from the pan and cool slightly.

2 Place the flour, sugar, eggs, yoghurt and butter in a bowl and beat for 5 minutes or until the mixture is smooth. Add the melted chocolate and mix well to combine.

3 Pour the mixture into a greased 23cm ring tin and bake for 50 minutes or until the cake is cooked when tested with a skewer. Stand the cake in the tin for 5 minutes before turning onto a wire rack to cool.

4 To make the icing, place the chocolate and cream in a heatproof bowl set over a saucepan of simmering water and heat, stirring, until the mixture is smooth. Spread the icing over the top and sides of the cake.

Chocolate-Pecan Gâteau

1 Place the egg yolks, sugar, and brandy in a bowl and beat until thick and pale. Place the egg whites in a clean bowl and beat until stiff peaks form. Fold the egg whites, pecans and flour into the egg yolk mixture.

2 Pour the mixture into a lightly greased and lined 23cm springform tin and bake for 40 minutes or until the cake is firm. Cool in the tin.

3 To make the glaze, place the chocolate, coffee powder, cream and brandy in a heatproof bowl set over a saucepan of simmering water and heat, stirring, until the mixture is smooth. Remove the bowl from the pan and set aside to cool slightly. Spread the glaze over the top and sides of the cooled cake. Sprinkle the pecans over the top of the cake and press into the side of the cake. Allow to set before serving.

4 eggs, separated

1 1/4 cups caster sugar

2 tbsp brandy

2 cups pecan nuts, roughly chopped

2 tbsp plain flour

Chocolate-Brandy Glaze

2 cups milk chocolate

2 tsp instant coffee powder

1/2 cup double cream

1 tbsp brandy

1 cup pecan nuts, roughly chopped

Oven temperature 160°C

serves 8

Almond Cake

1 cup plain flour
1 1/4 tsp baking powder
3/4 cup caster sugar
3 tbsp grated almonds
1 cup plain yoghurt
1 egg, beaten
1/2 cup safflower oil
1 tbsp dark rum
1 tsp grated lemon zest
whipped cream

For Brushing
1 tbsp apricot jam
2 tsp dark rum

Oven temperature 200°C

serves 4

1 Grease an 20cm round cake tin, cover the base with paper and the grease paper.

2 Sift together the flour and baking powder. In a bowl, combine them with the sugar and 1/2 the ground almonds.

3 Mix together the yoghurt, egg, oil, rum and lemon zest, and pour onto the flour. Stir until well combined.

4 Pour the mixture into the prepared pan. Sprinkle with the remaining almonds and bake in a preheated oven for 40–45 minutes.

5 Heat together the apricot jam and rum. When the cake is cooked and cooled a little, brush the mixture thickly over the top of the cake.

6 Serve cut into wedges with the whipped cream.

The Best Mud Cake

2¼ cups bittersweet chocolate, broken into pieces

1 cup icing sugar

¾ cup butter, chopped

5 eggs, separated

3 tbsp flour, sifted

cocoa powder, sifted

extra icing sugar, sifted, for dusting

Oven temperature 180°C

serves 10–12

1 Place the chocolate, sugar and butter in a heatproof bowl set over a saucepan of simmering water and heat, stirring, until the mixture is smooth. Remove the bowl and set aside to cool slightly. Beat in the egg yolks 1 at a time, beating well after each addition. Fold in the flour.

2 Place the egg whites in a clean bowl and beat until stiff peaks form. Fold the egg whites into the chocolate mixture. Pour the mixture into a greased 23cm springform tin and bake for 45 minutes or until the cake is cooked when tested with a skewer. Cool the cake in the pan.

3 Just prior to serving, dust the cake with the cocoa powder and icing sugar.

Arabian Date Cake

1 1/4 cups chopped dates

1 cup water

1 tsp instant coffee powder

1/2 cup margarine

1/2 cup brown sugar

1/5 cup honey

2 eggs

3/4 cup bittersweet chocolate, melted

2 cups plain flour, sifted

2 1/4 tsp baking powder

Oven temperature 180°C

serves 6–8

1 Combine the dates, water and coffee in a small saucepan, cook gently until the dates are tender and the liquid has been absorbed.

2 Mash the dates with a fork. Cream together the margarine, sugar and honey until light and creamy. Beat the eggs in, one at a time, beating well between each addition. Add the melted chocolate.

3 Fold in the sifted flour and baking powder with the date mixture. Mix well. Spoon the mixture into a lightly grease 10cm fluted cake pan. Bake in a pre-heated oven for 45–50 minutes or until cooked when tested.

4 Cool for 5 minutes in the pan. Serve warm or cold spread with margarine or coffee-flavoured cream cheese.

Profiteroles

1 Place the water and margarine in a saucepan and cook over gentle a heat until the margarine has melted and the water boils. Remove from the heat, add the sifted flour stir vigorously. Return to the heat and stir continuously until the mixture forms a ball around the spoon. Cool.

2 Gradually beat in the eggs, beating well after each addition. Place teaspoons of the mixture onto greased oven trays sprinkle with cold water.

3 Bake in a pre-heated oven for 10 minutes, reduce heat to 180°C and cook for a further 30 minutes or until the puffs are golden and fall lightly in the hand. Pierce the puffs to allow steam to escape. Cool in a draught-free place.

4 To make the filling, whip the cream to stiff stage, adding icing sugar and coffee liqueur. Fill the profiteroles. Spoon chocolate sauce on top to coat.

Pastry
1 cup water

4 tbsp margarine

1 cup plain, sifted

3 eggs, beaten

Filling
1 cup double cream

2 tbsp icing sugar

2 tsp coffee liqueur or

Chocolate Sauce
1 $^{1}/_{2}$ cups bittersweet chocolate

$^{1}/_{4}$ cup cream

Oven temperature 180°C

makes 20

Baked Double Cheese Cheesecake

Crumb Crust
2 1/2 cups sweet biscuit crumbs
1/2 cup margarine, melted
2 tsp hot water

Filling
1 1/2 cups cream cheese, softened
1 cup ricotta cheese
3/4 cup caster sugar
1 tsp vanilla extract
3 eggs
1 tbsp lemon juice

Topping
1 cup sour cream
1 tbsp caster sugar
3 tbsp toasted slivered almonds

Oven temperature 150°C

1 To make the crust, combine the biscuit crumbs, margarine and hot water. Mix well. Press the mixture onto the base and half way up the sides of a 23cm spring form cake tin. Refrigerate.

2 To make the filling, beat the cream cheese until smooth. Blend in the ricotta, sugar, vanilla extract, eggs, and lemon juice. Beat until well combined.

3 Pour the filling into the prepared crust. Bake in a preheated oven for 45 minutes.

4 To make the topping, combine the sour cream, sugar and almonds. Pour the topping over the filling and bake for a further 20 minutes. Cool in the pan. Refrigerate overnight before cutting.

serves 10

Raspberry-Cream Gâteau

1. Prepare the sponge mixture according to packet directions for mixing.

2. Cut a piece of greaseproof paper the same size as an 10cm spring form tin. Grease the base and sides lightly, place the circle of paper on the base, then grease the paper lightly. Pour the sponge mixture into the tin and cook in the oven for 15–20 minutes, or until the cake springs back when touched. Remove from the oven and place on the cake cooler and release spring clip on the pan and remove.

3. When the cake is cool, carefully cut into 4 even rounds. Mix the milk and tablespoon liqueur together and drizzle over the 4 sponge disks. Allow to stand 15–20 minutes.

4. Whip the cream until stiff and add 1 tablespoon of the liqueur. Place a sponge layer on a serving plate and spread with a layer of cream and raspberries. Place the second layer on top repeat until all the layers are used. Cover the top and sides with cream and garnish with the raspberries. Chill until ready to serve.

* Use rum or brandy in place of Kirsch or Cointreau. Layer and cover with chocolate or mocha butter cream garnish with almonds.

1 packet vanilla or chocolate sponge mix

1 cup milk

2 tbsp Kirsch or Cointreau liqueur

2 1/2 cups double cream

1 1/2 cups fresh or frozen raspberries

Oven temperature 180°C

serves 6

A squeeze of lemon juice added to double cream makes it whip faster. It's also a great idea to chill the beaters and mixing bowl first.

Lemon-Hazelnut Cake

¾ cup butter, softened

¾ cup caster sugar

1 cup plain flour

1 tsp baking powder

1 cup ground hazelnuts

3 eggs

¼ cup cream

Lemon Syrup

2 tsp grated lemon zest

juice of 2 lemons

½ cup caster sugar

Oven temperature 180°C

serves 6–8

1 Grease an 10cm fluted tube tin.

2 Place the butter, sugar, flour, baking powder, hazelnuts, eggs, and cream into a large bowl. Using an electric mixer, beat until smooth, for approximately 2–3 minutes.

3 Pour the mixture into a prepared cake tin and bake in a preheated oven for 40–45 minutes. Turn out onto a wire rack.

4 Place the cake on a cooling rack over a tray. Using a skewer, lightly prick the cake. Pour the hot lemon syrup evenly over the hot cake. Cool and serve with whipped cream if desired.

5 To make the lemon syrup, combine all the ingredients in a saucepan and stir over a low heat until the sugar is dissolved. Bring to the boil, remove from the heat and pour into a jug. Use as directed.

Freese swirls of fresh cream on a baking sheet. When frozen, transfer them carefully to a container for storage. Ideal for garnishing.

Mocha Walnut Cake

1 packet chocolate buttercake
2 eggs
2 tsp instant coffee powder
$^2/_3$ cup water
3 tbsp margarine
$^1/_4$ cup chopped walnuts

Coffee Glace Icing
1 tsp coffee powder
2 tsp of hot water
2 cups sifted icing sugar
1 tbsp margarine, softened

serves 6–8

1 Make up the cake as directed on the packet. Dissolve the coffee in the water and fold the margarine and walnuts through the cake batter after mixing. Spoon the mixture into a lightly greased 10cm fluted tube pan.

2 Bake in an oven for 40 minutes or until cooked when tested. Cool for 5 minutes in the pan before turning out. Cool.

3 Ice with coffee glace icing

4 To make the icing, disslove the coffee in the water. Blend into the icing sugar and margarine. Mix well.

Passionfruit Dessert Cake

½ cup margarine

¾ cup caster sugar

grated zest of 1 orange

2 eggs

1¼ cups plain, sifted

2 tsp baking powder

½ cup fresh passionfruit pulp

icing sugar

whipped cream

Passionfruit sauce

½ cup passionfruit pulp

1 tbsp icing sugar

1 tbsp orange juice

Oven temperature 180°C

serves 6

1 Cream together the margarine, sugar and orange zest. Beat in the eggs 1 at a time, beating well between each addition.

2 Fold in the sifted flour and baking powder, along with the passionfruit pulp. Spoon the mixture into a deep lightly greased 10cm round cake tin. Bake in a pre-heated oven for 40–45 minutes.

3 Serve warm, dusted with sifted icing sugar and accompanied by passionfruit sauce and whipped cream.

4 To make the sauce, combine passionfruit pulp, sugar and orange juice. Serve in a seperate bowl.

Fresh passionfruit may not always be readily available. Canned passionfruit pulp may be used iinstead. Most canned passsionfruit pulp is strained to remove the seeds, but it retains its flavour.

Sicilian Cassata Cake

1 Beat the eggs and sugar together with an electric mixer until thick and pale in colour. Fold in the sifted flour and baking powder.

2 Grease an 10cm cake tin and line the base with greased greaseproof paper cut to fit. Pour in the cake mixture and bake in a pre-heated hot oven, for 15–20 minutes. Cool completely.

3 To make the filling, beat the cheese and sugar together until light and fluffy. Stir in glace fruits, chocolate, nuts and liqueur. Refrigerate. Cut the cake into 2 layers. Place 1 layer in the base of cake tin in which it was cooked. Fill the centre with the cheese mixture. Cover with a second layer of cake. Refrigerate for 3 hours.

4 To make the icing, grate the chocolate coarsely and place it in a saucepan. Add the cream and heat very gently until the chocolate has melted. Turn the cake out onto a flat serving dish. Cover the top and sides with the chocolate icing and decorate with chocolate swirls.

Sponge

4 eggs & ¾ cup caster sugar

½ cup plain, sifted

1 ½ tsp baking powder

Filling

2 cups fresh ricotta cheese

¾ cup caster sugar

1 cup mixed glace fruit, chopped

⅔ cup bittersweet chocolate, chopped

1 tbsp chopped pistachio nuts

1 tbsp Maraschino liqueur

Chocolate Icing

2 cups bittersweet chocolate

½ cup cream

Oven temperature 200°C

serves 6–8

Apricot and Sultana Fruit Cake

2 cups dried apricots, chopped

1 1/4 cups sultanas

4 tbsp orange juice or orange liqueur

1 cup margarine

1 cup caster sugar

grated zest of 2 oranges

grated zest of 1 lemon

4 eggs

1 cup plain flour

1/2 tsp baking powder

1 cup almond meal or ground almonds

Oven temperature 160°C

serves 8–10

1 Combine the apricots, sultanas, and orange juice or liqueur in a bowl and set aside while preparing the cake batter.

2 Cream together the margarine, sugar and orange and lemon zest, until light and creamy. Beat in the eggs, 1 at a time, beating in well between each addition.

3 Sift the flour and baking powder, and fold into the creamed mixture.

4 Fold in the apricot mixture and almond meal. Spoon the cake batter into a lightly greased and paper lined 23cm round cake pan. Bake in a pre-heated for 1–1 1/2 hours or until cooked when tested. Cool in the pan.

The cake is best left uncut for 1–2 days.

Chocolate Roll

1 Place the egg yolks and sugar in a mixing bowl and beat until the mixture is thick and creamy. Beat in the chocolate, then fold in the flour mixture.

2 Beat the egg whites until stiff peaks form and fold into the chocolate mixture. Pour into a greased and lined 25 x 30cm Swiss roll tin and bake for 12–15 minutes or until just firm. Turn onto a damp teatowel sprinkled with sugar and roll up from the short end. Set aside to cool.

3 To make the filling, place the chocolate and cream in a small saucepan and cook over a low heat until the chocolate melts and the mixture is well blended. Bring to the boil, remove from the heat and set aside to cool completely. When cold, place in a mixing bowl over ice and beat until thick and creamy. Unroll the cake, spread with the filling and reroll. To serve, cut into slices.

A chocolate roll filled with chocolate cream makes a special afternoon tea treat or dessert. Irresistibly good to eat, these spectacular cakes are easy to make. Follow these step-by-step instructions for a perfect result every time.

5 eggs, separated

$1/4$ cup caster sugar

$3/4$ cup bittersweet chocolate, melted and cooled

2 tbsp plain flour, sifted with 2 tbsp cocoa powder and $1/4$ tsp baking powder

Chocolate Filling

$1/2$ cup bittersweet chocolate

$2/3$ cup double cream

Oven temperature 180°C

serves 8

Potato Scones

185g plain flour
1 tsp baking powder
1/2 tsp salt
1/2 cup margarine
2 eggs, beaten
3/8 cup milk
125g cold mashed potato
3 shallots, finely chopped
ground black pepper
flour, for kneading
butter, for spreading

Oven temperature 230°C

serves 6–8

1 Sift the flour, baking powder and salt together, then rub in the margarine. Beat the eggs and milk together and add to flour mixture to make a firm dough.

2 Add finely mashed potatoes, shallots and pepper. Stir through lightly. Turn onto a floured board or sheet of non-stick oven paper, knead, then roll out to 1cm/1/2 in thickness. Cut into rounds and bake in 230°C oven for 30 minutes. Split open while hot and spread with butter and serve.

Cheese & Bacon Damper

1 Rub the margarine into the flour until mixture resembles coarse breadcrumbs.

2 Stir in parsley, chives, cheese and bacon, mix well.

3 Combine the egg and milk, stir into the dry ingredients and mix to a soft dough.

4 Turn dough onto a lightly floured board and knead lightly.

5 Shape into a cob, cut a deep cross in the centre of the cob and place on a sheet of baking paper on an oven tray.

6 Bake in the oven at 200°C for 30 minutes or until hollow-sounding when tapped underneath.

7 Serve hot with a crock of butter on a buffet table, cut into small pieces.

---

3 tbsp margarine or butter

2 1/2 cups self-raising flour

2 tsp parsley flakes

1 tsp chopped chives

1 cup grated tasty (mature Cheddar) cheese

2 rashers cooked bacon, finely chopped

1 egg

3/4 cup milk

Oven temperature 200°C

serves 6–8

Cornbread

125g sifted plain flour
4 tsp baking powder
¾ tsp salt
30g sugar
125g yellow cornmeal
2 eggs
1 cup milk
30g butter
butter, to serve

Oven temperature 220°C

serves 4

1 Sift flour with baking powder and salt. Stir in sugar and cornmeal. Add eggs, milk and melted butter. Beat until just smooth.

2 Pour into a 23x23x5cm tin lined with baking paper and bake in 220°C oven for 20–25 minutes.

3 Remove from tin and cut into squares to serve with butter.

Cheese & Onion Scones

500g self-raising flour

1 tsp salt

1/4 tsp cayenne pepper

60g margarine or butter

100g grated cheese

1 tbsp finely chopped parsley

1 dessertspoon finely chopped onion

1 egg, beaten

1 1/2 cups milk

Oven temperature 230°C

serves 6

1 Sift flour, salt and cayenne. Rub margarine or butter into flour. Add grated cheese, parsley and onion and mix well.

2 Make a well in the centre and add beaten egg and milk all at once, and mix quickly to a soft dough. Turn out on a floured board and knead just enough to make a smooth surface.

3 Roll to 1cm thickness and cut into rounds. Place on a floured tray, glaze tops with milk or beaten egg and milk. Bake in a hot oven 230°C for 10–15 minutes or until scones are browned.

Scones

2 cups self-raising flour
1 tsp baking powder
2 tsp sugar
45g butter
1 egg
½ cup milk

Oven temperature 220°C

makes 12

1   Sift together flour and baking powder into a large bowl. Stir in sugar, then rub in butter, using fingertips, until mixture resembles coarse breadcrumbs.

2   Whisk together egg and milk. Make a well in centre of flour mixture, pour in egg mixture and mix to form a soft dough. Turn onto a lightly floured surface and knead lightly.

3   Press dough out to a 2cm thickness, using palm of hand. Cut out scones using a floured 5cm cutter. Avoid twisting the cutter, or the scones will rise unevenly.

4   Arrange scones close together on a greased and lightly floured baking tray or in a shallow 20cm round cake tin. Brush with a little milk and bake for 12–15 minutes or until golden.

To grease and flour a cake tin or baking tray, lightly brush with melted butter or margarine, then sprinkle with flour and shake to coat evenly. Invert on work surface and tap gently to remove excess flour.

Bacon Cornbread Pots

1 Cook bacon in a nonstick frying pan over a medium heat for 3–4 minutes or until crisp. Remove bacon from pan and drain on absorbent kitchen paper.

2 Place cornmeal (polenta), flour, baking powder, sugar, salt, Parmesan cheese and butter in a food processor and process until mixture resembles fine breadcrumbs.

3 Combine eggs and milk and, with machine running, pour into cornmeal (polenta) mixture and process until combined and batter is smooth. Take care not to overmix. Stir in bacon.

4 Spoon batter into three medium-sized terracotta flowerpots lined with well-greased aluminium foil. Place on a baking tray and bake for 25–30 minutes or until golden.

Cooked in flowerpots these tasty cornbread loaves are a perfect accompaniment to soup or salad. Remember that the size of the flowerpots you use will determine the number of loaves you produce.

4 rashers bacon, finely chopped

1 1/2 cups fine cornmeal (polenta)

1 cup plain flour

2 1/2 tsp baking powder

4 tsp sugar

1/2 tsp salt

60g grated Parmesan cheese

90g butter, chopped

2 eggs, lightly beaten

1 1/4 cups buttermilk or milk

Oven temperature 200°C

serves 6

* makes 3 medium-sized flowerpot loaves

Index

Almond Cake	78	Cheese and Onion Scones	93	Low Fat Cottage Cheese Muffins	12	Rock Cakes	70
Almond Cherry Cake	60	Cheese Muffins	9	Macaroon Cake	54	Satay Muffins	21
Apple & Bran Muffins	28	Choc-Rough Muffins	41	Mango Bran Muffins	47	Scones	94
Apple Crumble Dessert Cake	49	Chocolate Apple Streudel Cake	65	Mexican Muffins	13	Sesameal Muffins	22
Apricot Oat-Bran Muffins	29	Chocolate Espresso Cheesecake	75	Mini Sardine Muffins	27	Sicilian Cassarta Cake	87
Apricote and Sultana Fruit Cake	88	Chocolate Hazelnut Torte	74	Mocha Walnut Cake	85	Simple Chocolate Cake	71
Arabian Date Cake	80	Chocolate Macaroon Cake	67	Moroccan Couscous Muffins	14	Sticky Date Muffins	43
Bacon Cornbread Pots	95	Chocolate Mousse Cake	69	Mushroom Muffins	26	Sundried Tomato and	
Baked Double		Chocolate Pecan Gateau	77	Never Fail Sponge	51	Basil Pesto Muffins	23
Cheese Cheesecake	82	Chocolate Pound Cake	73	Oat Bran Fruit Muffins	27	Swedish Potato Muffins	24
Banana and Mango Muffins	34	Chocolate Roll	89	Olive and Feta Muffins	15	Sweet Potato Muffins	42
Banana Cake	63	Chocolate Rum and Raisin Cake	66	Olive Tapenade and		The Best Mudcake	79
Banana Choc0Chip Muffins	44	Classic Blueberry Muffins	45	Anchovy Muffins	16	Tomato and basil Muffins	25
Beer Muffins	6	Cornbread Muffins	30	Orange Sugar Cube Muffins	40	Tosca cake	56
Blackberry & Apple Muffins	33	Cornbread	92	Passionfruit Dessert cake	86	Walnut and Blue Cheese Muffins	10
Blackberry Muffins with		Fruit Cake	50	Pineapple & Coconut Muffins	39	White Chocolate Yoghurt Cake	76
Yummy Blackberry Cream	35	Gingerbread	53	Pistachio Muffins	17	Wholemeal Apple Cake	55
Blackberry Spice Muffins	46	Grandma's Chocolate Cake	72	Pizza Muffins	18		
Bowls Cake	61	Honey and Fig Muffins	36	Ploughman's Muffins	19		
Café Cup Cake	68	Honey Cake	62	Potato Scons	90		
Cappuccino Muffins	38	Honey, Bran and walnut Muffins	37	Potato Sour-Cream Muffins	31		
Carrot and Coriander Muffins	7	John's Caper Muffins	11	Profiteroles	81		
Cathedredal Window Cakes	57	Lemon Hazelnut Cake	84	Raisin and Lemon Cake	58		
Cheese and bacon Damper	91	Lemon Poppy Seed Muffins	48	Raspberry Cream gateau	83		
Cheese and Bacon Muffins	32	Lemon Sour Cream Cake	64	Rich Chocolate Cake	52		
Cheese and Cornmeal Muffins	8	Linzer Cake	59	Roasted capsicum Muffins	20		